THE

Chanukah Activity

BOOK

✦ JUDY DICK ✦

UAHC Press • New York, New York

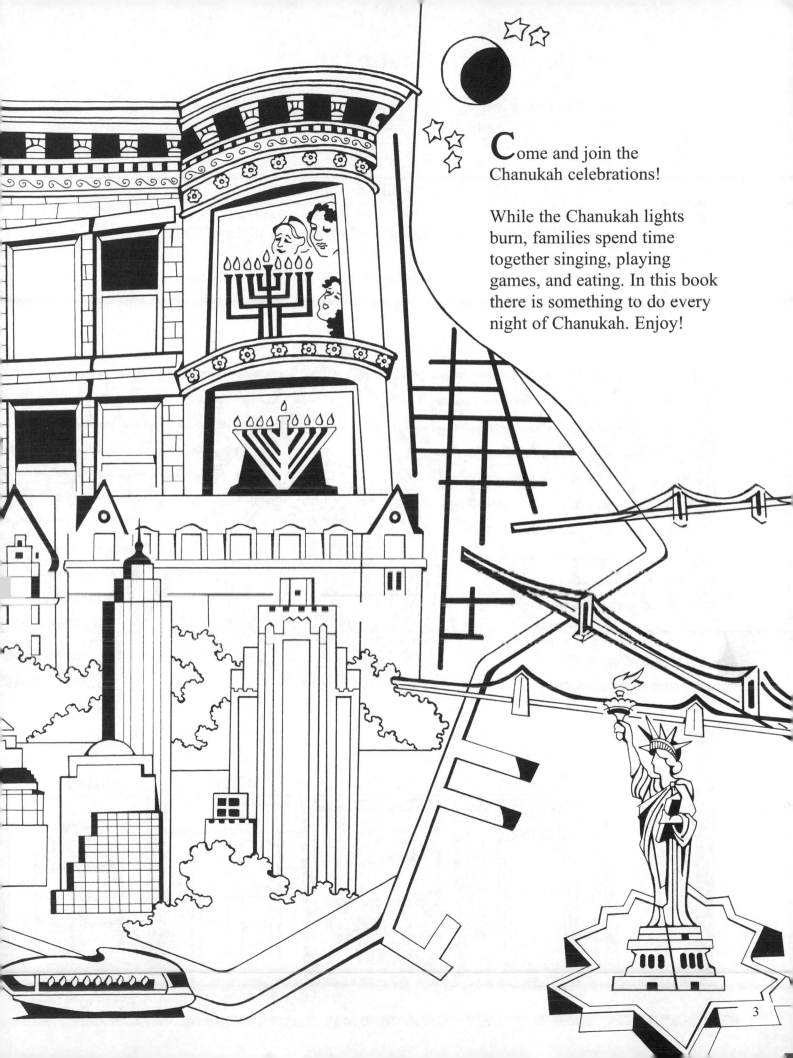

Come and join the Chanukah celebrations!

While the Chanukah lights burn, families spend time together singing, playing games, and eating. In this book there is something to do every night of Chanukah. Enjoy!

3

At Home with Chanukah

On Chanukah we light a *chanukiyah*. As night falls and the stars come out, get ready to light your own.

Chanukah How-To:
Each night of Chanukah, we add an additional flame, starting from the right and moving to the left. We light from left to right.
   Draw a new candle and flame below on each night of Chanukah.

A helper candle, called a *shamash,* is used to light the flames.

SHAMASH

NIGHT 8   NIGHT 7   NIGHT 6   NIGHT 5

Chanukah Candle Blessing

בָּרוּךְ אַתָּה יי אֱלֹהֵינוּ
מֶלֶךְ הָעוֹלָם, אֲשֶׁר
קִדְּשָׁנוּ בְּמִצְוֹתָיו וְצִוָּנוּ
לְהַדְלִיק נֵר שֶׁל חֲנֻכָּה.

Baruch atah Adonai, Eloheinu melech haolam asher kid'shanu b'mitzvotav v'tzivanu l'hadlik ner shel Chanukah.

We praise You, Eternal God, Sovereign of the universe:
You hallow us with Your mitzvot and command us to kindle the Chanukah lights.

(For the other blessings said on Chanukah, see page 27.)

Design your own window!

NIGHT 4   NIGHT 3   NIGHT 2   NIGHT 1

5

Chanukah History

Many years ago, most Jews lived in the country of Israel, then called Judea. Its capital was the city of Jerusalem, and in it was the holiest place in the land, the Temple.

In 332 B.C.E., the powerful conqueror Alexander the Great marched into Judea and took over. He made Judea part of the Greek empire. New ideas from the Greeks came to the Jewish people. In the beginning, the Jews could choose to learn both Greek ideas and also continue to follow the Torah.

In 175 B.C.E., the emperor Antiochus IV came to the throne. He wanted to make Jerusalem a Greek city and turn the Holy Temple into a temple for Greek gods. He forbade the Jews from keeping their traditions and tried to force them to be Greek. He made many new rules.

Write down a good rule. Why is it a good rule?

_____

Write down a bad rule. Why is it a bad rule?

_____

Some of Antiochus' rules were:	Why do you think they are bad rules?
No celebration of Shabbat and Jewish holidays.	_____
No circumcision.	_____
No studying the Torah.	_____
Worship Greek gods.	_____

How do you think it would have felt to be a Jew at this time?

_____

Meet the Characters

The Jews reacted in different ways. Some wanted to forget about being Jewish and were happy to be like the Greeks. Others gave in to the Greeks out of fear. But one family of priests refused to allow Judaism to be destroyed. This was the Hasmonean family, led by Mattathias the father and his five sons.

Imagine a meeting between the Hasmoneans and Antiochus. How could they convince him to allow the Jews to keep their traditions? Write in the conversation in the bubbles above the characters' heads.

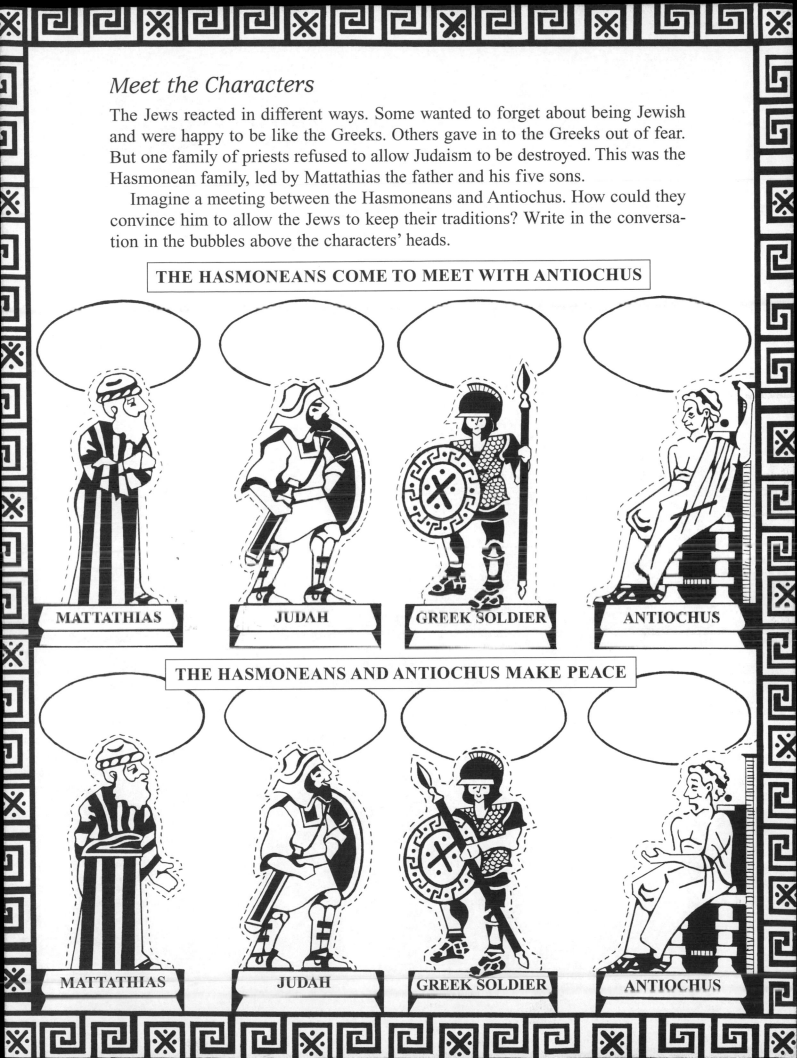

THE HASMONEANS COME TO MEET WITH ANTIOCHUS

MATTATHIAS   JUDAH   GREEK SOLDIER   ANTIOCHUS

THE HASMONEANS AND ANTIOCHUS MAKE PEACE

MATTATHIAS   JUDAH   GREEK SOLDIER   ANTIOCHUS

Jerusalem Ahead

Mattathias and his sons fought bravely against the Greek armies. Before he died, Mattathias appointed his son Judah to lead the Jewish army. Judah led the small army, known as the Maccabees, in surprise attacks against the stronger Greek armies. They won battle after battle.

The Maccabees fought so that they could be free. Use your knowledge of Judaism to help them win their freedom and reach Jerusalem!

After 3 years of battles, the Greeks were weakened and stopped fighting. The Maccabees immediately headed to Jerusalem and retook the city in 164 B.C.E.

Game of Knowledge

Instructions

1. To make a **game piece**, turn back a page and cut out a character. Fold the bottom so that it stands up. Now color it in!

2. To make **game cards,** turn to the page after the game board. Trace the shape and write in your own questions or use the questions provided. Color the cards.

3. **To play,** turn to the game board. Place your piece in a starter square (look for the arrows). Take turns asking each other questions from the cards. When you get a question right, you may move to another square diagonally. If there is a Greek in the way, you must jump over him, but to do this you must answer 2 questions! **Whoever reaches the entrance of Jerusalem first wins!**

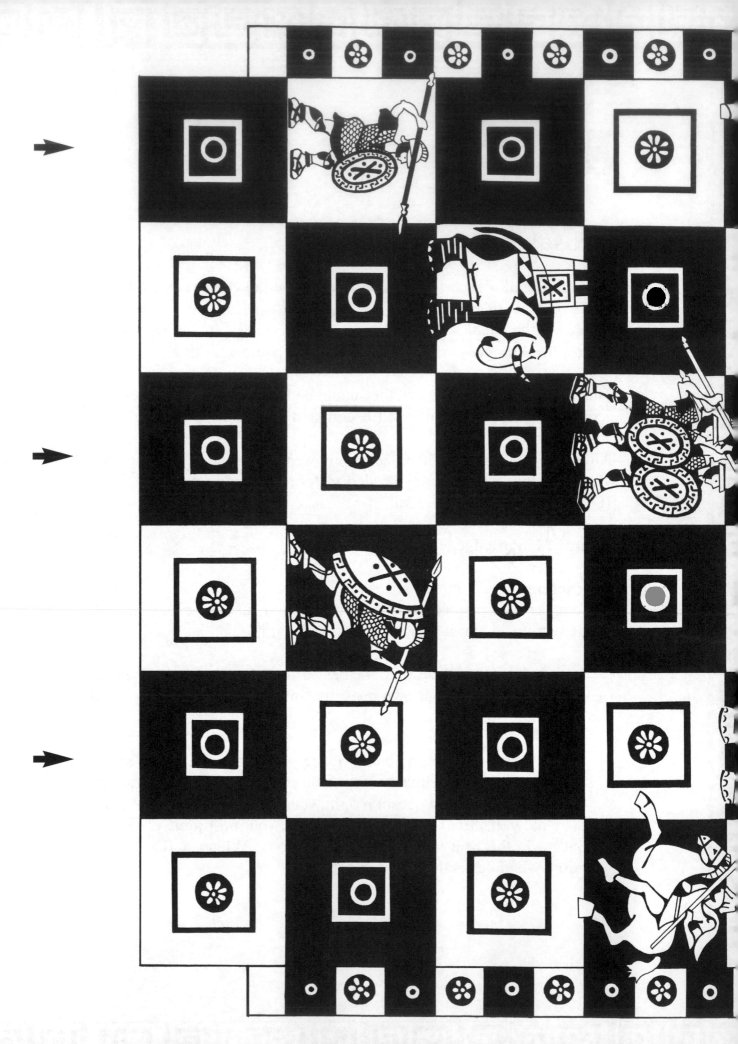

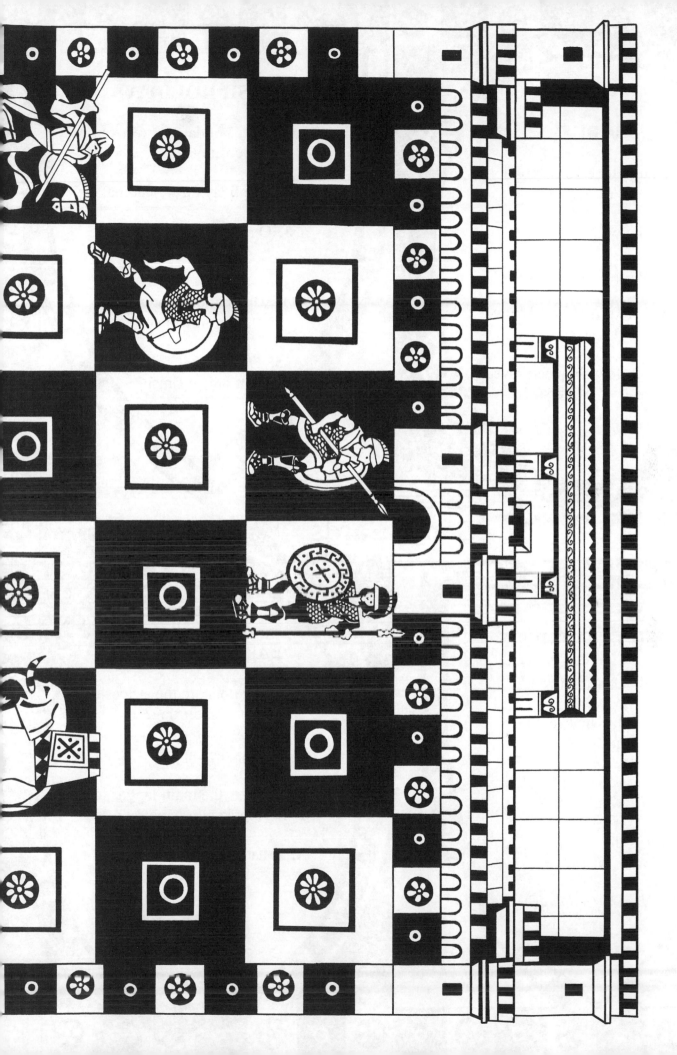

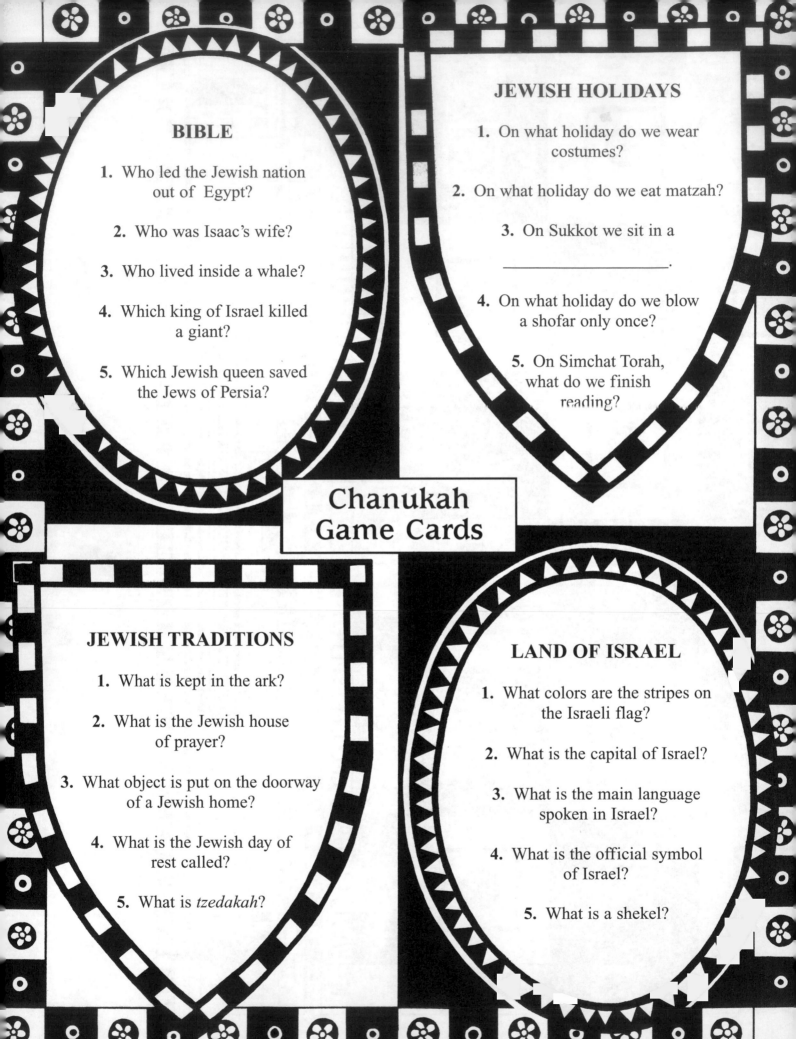

BIBLE

1. Who led the Jewish nation out of Egypt?

2. Who was Isaac's wife?

3. Who lived inside a whale?

4. Which king of Israel killed a giant?

5. Which Jewish queen saved the Jews of Persia?

JEWISH HOLIDAYS

1. On what holiday do we wear costumes?

2. On what holiday do we eat matzah?

3. On Sukkot we sit in a

_____.

4. On what holiday do we blow a shofar only once?

5. On Simchat Torah, what do we finish reading?

Chanukah Game Cards

JEWISH TRADITIONS

1. What is kept in the ark?

2. What is the Jewish house of prayer?

3. What object is put on the doorway of a Jewish home?

4. What is the Jewish day of rest called?

5. What is *tzedakah*?

LAND OF ISRAEL

1. What colors are the stripes on the Israeli flag?

2. What is the capital of Israel?

3. What is the main language spoken in Israel?

4. What is the official symbol of Israel?

5. What is a shekel?

TIMES OF THE BIBLE

JERUSALEM, Holiday of Sukkot,
11th year of King Solomon's rule, month of Cheshvan

Weather: Today, mostly sunny and clear, some clouds due to Temple dedication.

First Temple Dedicated in Jerusalem!

Crowds Attend Temple Dedication

By Joseph son of Aaron

Thousands streamed to the holy city of Jerusalem to be part of the *Chanukat HaBayit,* the dedication ceremony for the Temple. King Solomon finally finished building the Temple after 7 years. The white and gold Temple dazzled all who saw it. The whole nation joined the king in offering prayers and sacrifices on the altar to God. The celebrations lasted for 14 days, after which everyone returned home.

UNSCRAMBLE: What They Saw

1. RAATL _____

2. RAK _____

3. NOOSLOM _____

5. EPLTME _____

5. NMKOIHA _____

THE HOLY ARK:
A Special Report
By Binyamin HaLevi

The Ark, made for Moses in the desert, was of gold and wood. The *kohanim* (priests) carried it into the Temple. Color in the pieces with dots in them to see the Ark. What was kept inside it?

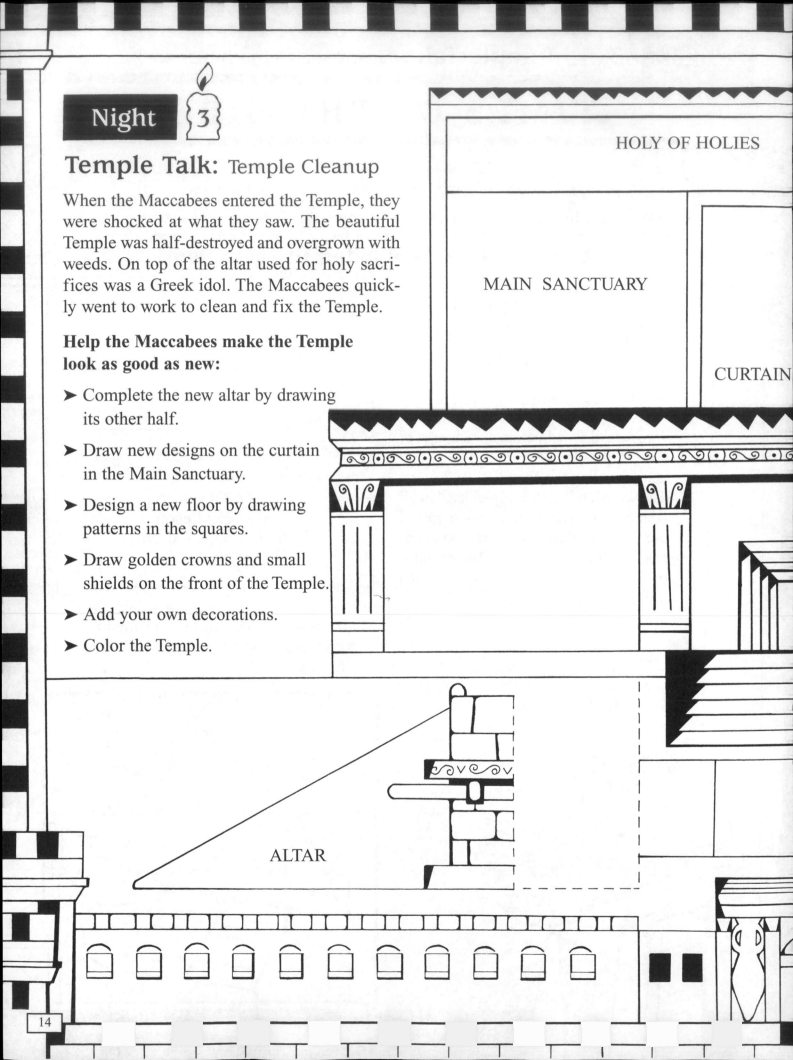

Night 3

Temple Talk: Temple Cleanup

When the Maccabees entered the Temple, they were shocked at what they saw. The beautiful Temple was half-destroyed and overgrown with weeds. On top of the altar used for holy sacrifices was a Greek idol. The Maccabees quickly went to work to clean and fix the Temple.

Help the Maccabees make the Temple look as good as new:

➤ Complete the new altar by drawing its other half.

➤ Draw new designs on the curtain in the Main Sanctuary.

➤ Design a new floor by drawing patterns in the squares.

➤ Draw golden crowns and small shields on the front of the Temple.

➤ Add your own decorations.

➤ Color the Temple.

HOLY OF HOLIES

MAIN SANCTUARY

CURTAIN

ALTAR

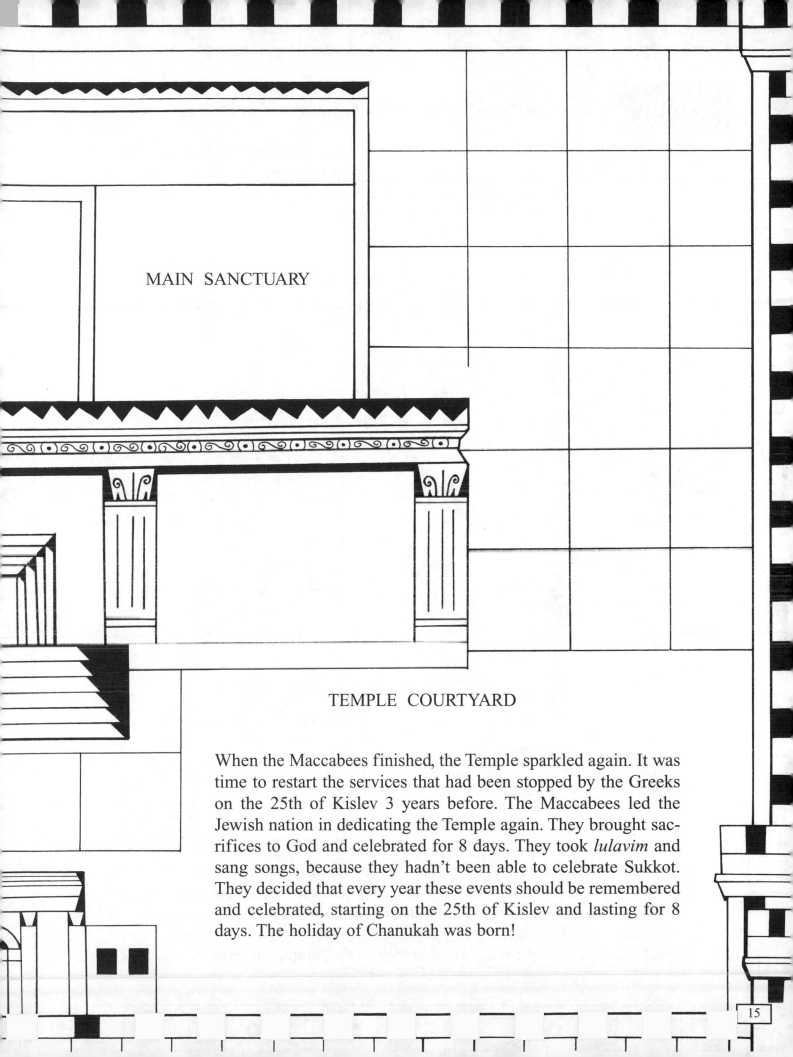

MAIN SANCTUARY

TEMPLE COURTYARD

When the Maccabees finished, the Temple sparkled again. It was time to restart the services that had been stopped by the Greeks on the 25th of Kislev 3 years before. The Maccabees led the Jewish nation in dedicating the Temple again. They brought sacrifices to God and celebrated for 8 days. They took *lulavim* and sang songs, because they hadn't been able to celebrate Sukkot. They decided that every year these events should be remembered and celebrated, starting on the 25th of Kislev and lasting for 8 days. The holiday of Chanukah was born!

Night {3} Temple Talk: Flashback to Lights

In the Temple of King Solomon stood the menorah, a seven branched lamp made of pure gold. Every night it would be lit using only the purest olive oil. The Maccabees had to make a new menorah. See the menorah below and draw it in the main sanctuary of the Temple on the previous page.

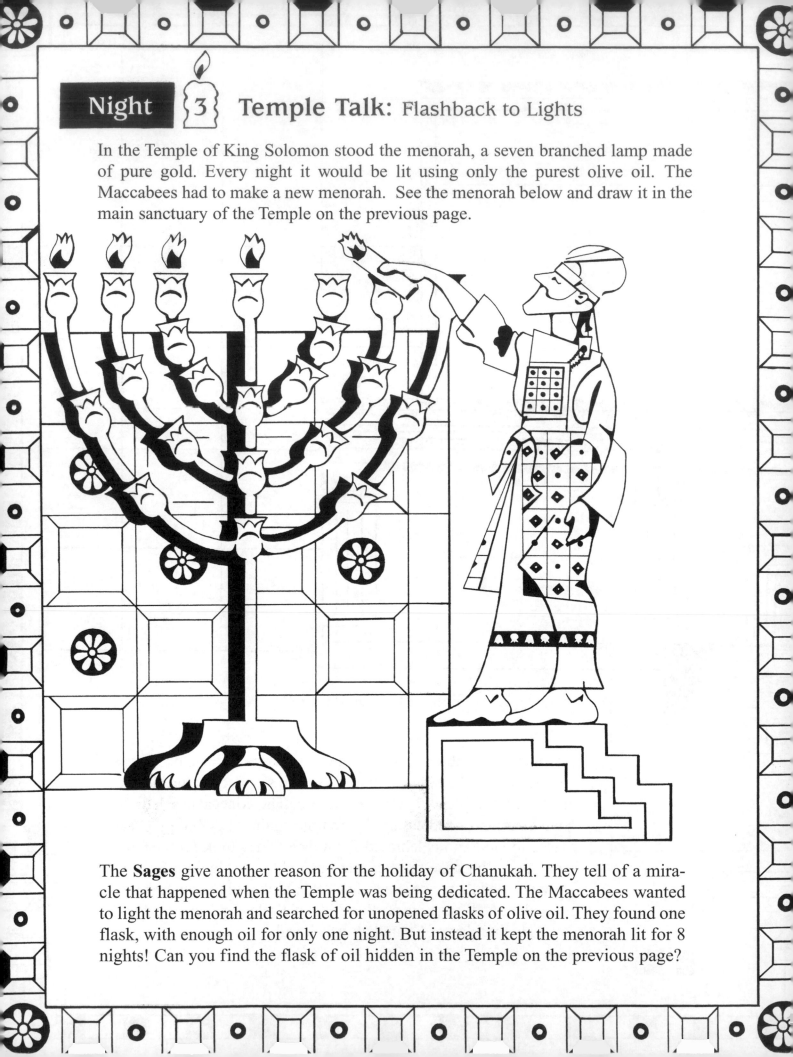

The **Sages** give another reason for the holiday of Chanukah. They tell of a miracle that happened when the Temple was being dedicated. The Maccabees wanted to light the menorah and searched for unopened flasks of olive oil. They found one flask, with enough oil for only one night. But instead it kept the menorah lit for 8 nights! Can you find the flask of oil hidden in the Temple on the previous page?

For the **Sages,** the miracle of lights was the most important part of Chanukah. In order to remind us of this miracle, they decided that we too should light a lamp on Chanukah. Two Sages, **Hillel** and **Shammai,** had a debate about how many lights should be lit each night. Find out what they did. Each has just lit his *chanukiyah* on the first night of Chanukah.

HILLEL: On each night of Chanukah an extra light should be lit. Let's keep adding light!

How many lights did Hillel light on the first night? _____ How many will he have to light on the 8th night? _____

Draw them in his lamp below.

What do you think is his reason? _____

SHAMMAI: On each night of Chanukah we should count down and light one light less.

How many lights did Shammai light on the first night? _____ How many will he have to light on the 8th night? _____

Draw them in his lamp below.

What do you think is his reason?

_____

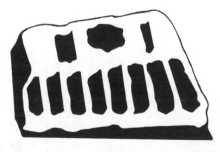

Do you agree with Hillel or Shammai? Why?

_____.

Whom do you think won the debate?

_____.

Night 4   Chanukah Highlights

Since the time of Hillel, Jews have been adding an extra light each night of Chanukah, ending with eight lights on the last night. They use both olive oil and candles to light the *chanukiyah*. As Jews moved from place to place they continued to light candles, but the *chanukiyot* they made and used looked very different.

USA

GERMANY

HOLLAND

FRANCE

MOROCCO

The *chanukiyot* were lit in a place where people could see them and remember the miracles that happened to the Maccabees. They were placed on or next to the door of a house, outside at the entrance, or in front of a window.

Travel around the world on Chanukah! How many kinds of *chanukiyot* can you find?

Find and color a *chanukiyah*:

1. … in the shape of a triangle.
2. … decorated with hand shapes (called *hamsa*).
3. … that looks like the Temple menorah because it has branches. (How many does this lamp have?)
4. … decorated with hearts.
5. … decorated with roosters.
6. … inside a wooden house. It has two candleholders on either side. Can you guess why?
7. … that looks like a brick wall.
8. … being lit by Hillel.

Bonus: Find the Statue of Liberty.

POLAND

ITALY

ISRAEL

IRAQ

After we light the *chanukiyah,* we celebrate by singing songs. One of the oldest songs for Chanukah, "Maoz Tzur," was written about seven hundred years ago!

Each part of "Maoz Tzur" tells of a different event in Jewish history. Each time, a nation tried to destroy the Jewish people but was defeated. Complete the sentences below by writing in the correct name of each nation, found on the timeline underneath the pictures. Then match each picture to its nation by drawing a line from the picture to the name on the timeline.

The _____ tried to control the Land of Israel and force the Jews to follow their way of life, but were defeated by the Maccabees.

The _____ destroyed the First Temple and moved the Jewish nation to Babylon. They were allowed to return to the Land of Israel after seventy years.

The _____ forced the Israelites to work as slaves, but God split the Red Sea, bringing the Israelites to freedom.

Haman convinced the _____ to allow him to destroy the Jews, but the Jewish leader Mordechai spoiled his plans and saved the nation.

EGYPTIANS

BABYLONIANS

עוז צור ישועתי

מָעוֹז צוּר יְשׁוּעָתִי,

לְךָ נָאֶה לְשַׁבֵּחַ,

תִּכּוֹן בֵּית תְּפִלָּתִי,

וְשָׁם תּוֹדָה נְזַבֵּחַ.

לְעֵת תָּכִין מַטְבֵּחַ,

מִצָּר הַמְנַבֵּחַ,

אָז אֶגְמוֹר, בְּשִׁיר מִזְמוֹר,

חֲנֻכַּת הַמִּזְבֵּחַ.

Rock of Ages

Rock of ages, let our song
Praise Your saving power;
You, amid the raging foes,
Were our sheltering tower.
Furious, they assailed us
But Your arm availed us,
And Your word
Broke their sword,
When our own strength
    failed us.

*Maoz tzur y'shuati l'cha na-eh
    l'shabei-ach,
tikon beit t'filati v'sham todah
    n'zabei-ach.
L'eit tashbit matbei-ach v'tzar
    ham'nabei-ach,
az egmor, b'shir mizmor
    chanukat hamizbei-ach.*

ביר קדשו הביאני

רות קומת ברוש בקש

PERSIANS

GREEKS

• Latkes •

We also celebrate Chanukah by cooking and eating special food. Many Chanukah dishes are made with an ingredient that reminds us of one of the miracles. What do you think the ingredient is? These popular Chanukah recipes from around the world both contain this ingredient.

The secret ingredient is: _____ .

Try my crispy potato pancakes, called latkes.

For my recipe, go to page 31.

· Birmuelos ·

Try my doughnuts, called *birmuelos* in Ladino or *sufganiyòt* in Hebrew.

For my recipe, go to page 31.

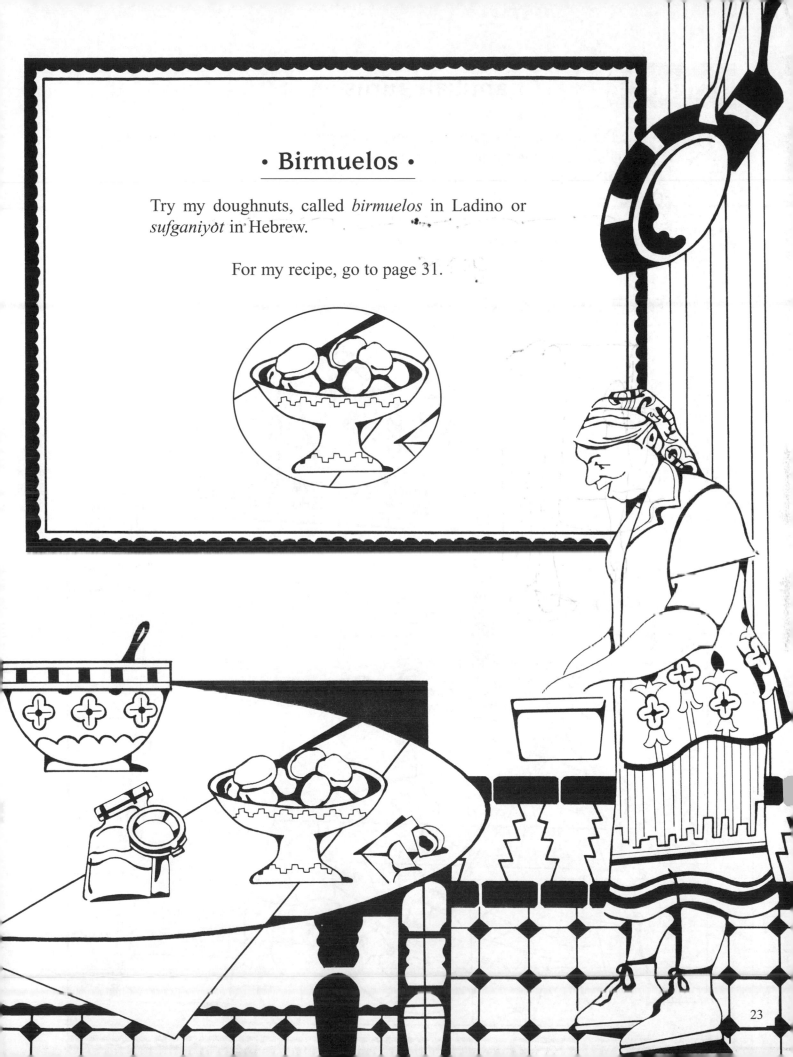

While the candles burn, families celebrate by playing games and exchanging gifts. Discover what are in the gifts below.

Gift 1: Draw in your own gift.

Gift 2: Find the following words:

bicycle, bow, sweater, watch, chocolate, book, doll, bear, kite

Gift 3: Color in the shapes with dots.

What is inside? guitar

The Dreidel Game

4. ש ___
Sham
(There)
Add coin or
nut to the pot.

3. יה ___
Hayah
(Happened)
Take half of
the pot.

The dreidel is a spinning top that has Hebrew letters on it. The letters hint at a Chanukah message. Find each letter by coloring in the shapes with dots in each dreidel. Then complete the Hebrew words and write them in the spaces below to find out the whole message.

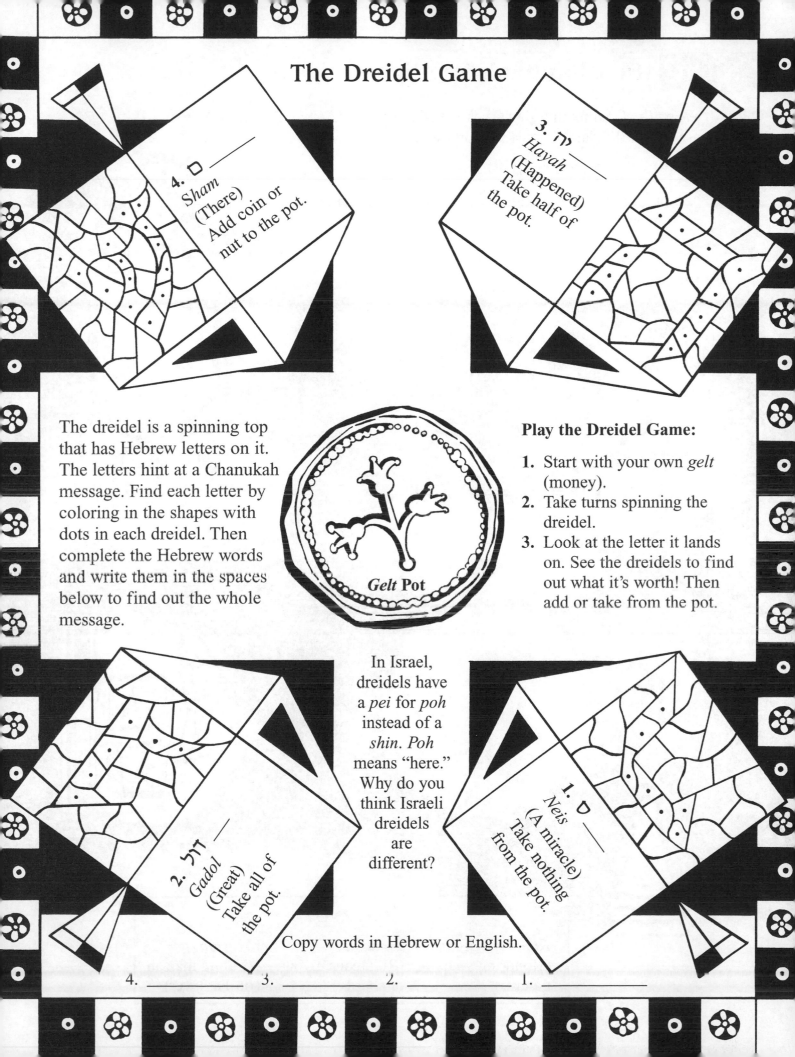

Gelt Pot

Play the Dreidel Game:

1. Start with your own *gelt* (money).
2. Take turns spinning the dreidel.
3. Look at the letter it lands on. See the dreidels to find out what it's worth! Then add or take from the pot.

In Israel, dreidels have a *pei* for *poh* instead of a *shin*. *Poh* means "here." Why do you think Israeli dreidels are different?

2. גד ___
Gadol
(Great)
Take all of
the pot.

1. ש ___
Neis
(A miracle)
Take nothing
from the pot.

Copy words in Hebrew or English.

4. _____ 3. _____ 2. _____ 1. _____

When the Chanukah lights are finished burning and Chanukah is over, we are left in the dark to start the long winter.

" כִּי נֵר מִצְוָה, וְתוֹרָה אוֹר. "

"For a *mitzvah* [commandment] is a lamp, and Torah is light."
Proverbs 6:23

What is another way to bring light into the world?

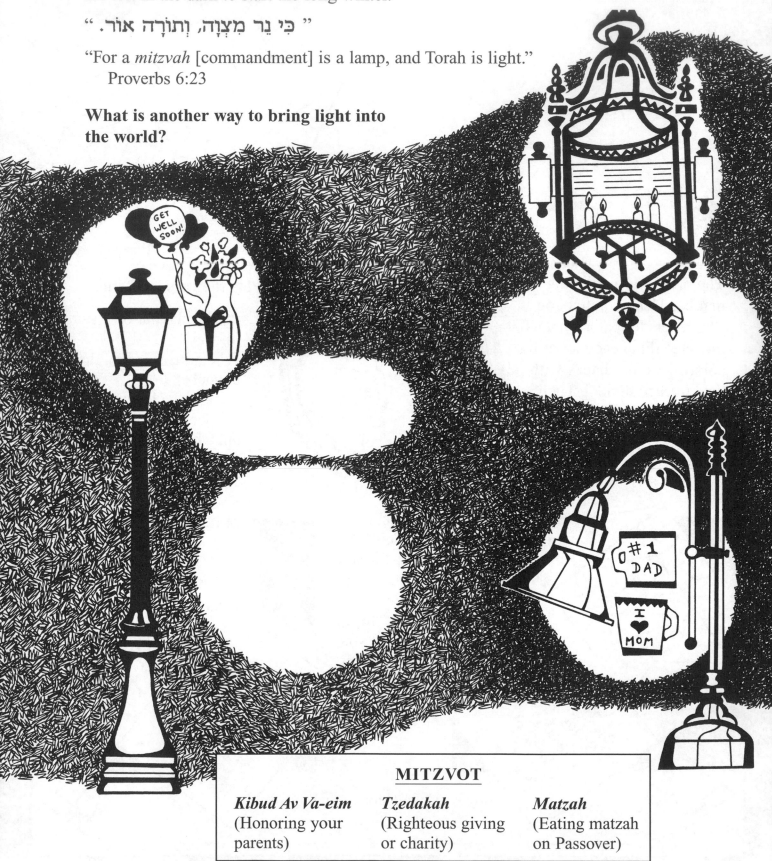

MITZVOT

Kibud Av Va-eim	*Tzedakah*	*Matzah*
(Honoring your parents)	(Righteous giving or charity)	(Eating matzah on Passover)

Each lamp below teaches a different mitzvah. Write the name of the mitzvah next to its picture in the halo of light. Choose from the mitzvot in the box below. In the empty halos, draw in your own mitzvot.

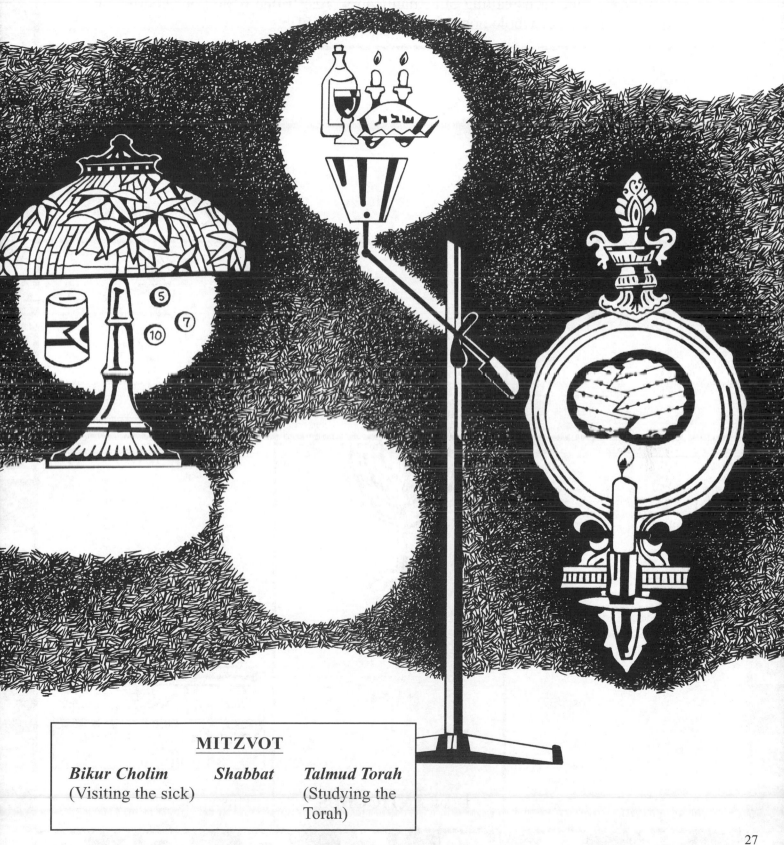

MITZVOT

Bikur Cholim
(Visiting the sick)

Shabbat

Talmud Torah
(Studying the Torah)

Chanukah Bingo

How much did you learn about Chanukah? Test your knowledge with one last game, **Chanukah Bingo**. Complete the bingo board below. Copy the board for others, and in the blank squares make your own Chanukah clues.

How to play: Take turns calling out Chanukah words. If one is on your board, cover the square. When your whole board is covered, you win!

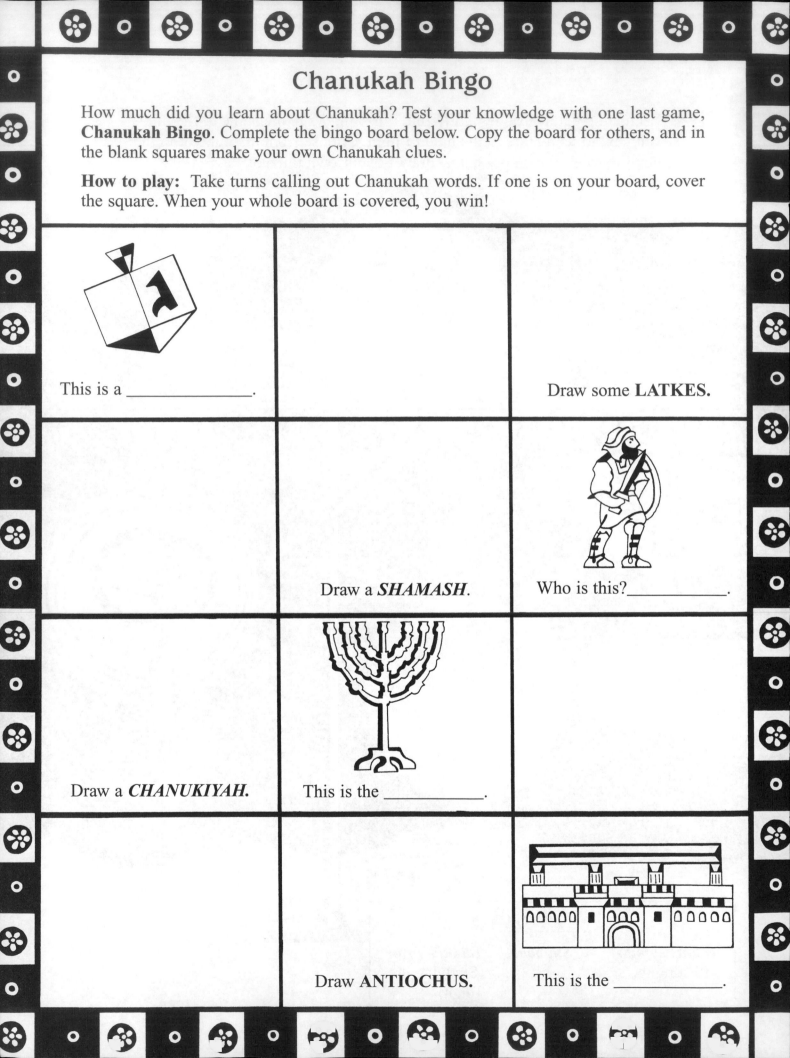

This is a _____.

Draw some **LATKES.**

Draw a *SHAMASH*.

Who is this? _____.

Draw a *CHANUKIYAH.*

This is the _____.

Draw **ANTIOCHUS.**

This is the _____.

Additional Chanukah Blessings

For every night of Chanukah:

Baruch atah Adonai, Eloheinu melech haolam, she'aseh nisim la-avoteiu / l'imoteinu bayamin haheim bazman hazeh.

בָּרוּךְ אַתָּה יי אֱלֹהֵינוּ
מֶלֶךְ הָעוֹלָם, שֶׁעָשָׂה נִסִּים
לַאֲבוֹתֵֽינוּ/לְאִמּוֹתֵֽינוּ
בַּיָּמִים הָהֵם בַּזְּמַן הַזֶּה.

We praise You, Eternal God, Sovereign of the universe: You showed wonders to our ancestors in days of old, at this season.

For the first night only:

Baruch atah Adonai, Eloheinu melech haolam, shehechiyanu, v'kiyemanu, v'higi-anu lazman hazeh.

בָּרוּךְ אַתָּה יי אֱלֹהֵינוּ
מֶלֶךְ הָעוֹלָם, שֶׁהֶחֱיָֽנוּ
וְקִיְּמָֽנוּ וְהִגִּיעָֽנוּ
לַזְּמַן הַזֶּה.

We praise You, Eternal God, Sovereign of the universe, for giving us life, for sustaining us, and for enabling us to reach this season.

ANSWER KEY

Page 12

Bible
1. Moses
2. Rebekah
3. Jonah
4. David
5. Esther

Jewish Traditions
1. Torah scroll
2. synagogue
3. mezuzah
4. Shabbat
5. righteous giving or charity

Jewish Holidays
1. Purim
2. Passover
3. sukkah
4. Yom Kippur
5. Torah

Land of Israel
1. blue
2. Jerusalem
3. Hebrew
4. menorah
5. Israeli money / coin

Page 13

Unscramble
1. altar
2. ark
3. Solomon
4. Temple
5. *Kohanim*

Page 17

How many lights did Hillel light on the first night? <u>One.</u>
How many will he have to light on the eighth night? <u>Eight.</u>
How many lights did Shammai light on the first night? <u>Eight.</u>
How many will he have to light on the eighth night? <u>One.</u>
Whom do you think won the debate? <u>Hillel.</u>

Pages 18–19

Chanukah Highlights
1. France, 14th century
2. Iraq, 19th century
3. Germany, 17th century
4. Holland, 18th century
5. Morocco, 19th century
6. For use as Shabbat candles;
   Poland, 18th century
7. Italy, 16th century
8. Jerusalem, Israel

Pages 20–21

"Maoz Tzur"
The <u>Greeks</u> tried to control…
The <u>Babylonians</u> destroyed the First…
The <u>Egyptians</u> forced the Israelites…
Haman convinced the <u>Persians</u> to allow
   him to …

Page 22
The secret ingredient is <u>oil</u>.

Latkes

1 large onion	salt and pepper
7 medium potatoes	½ cup matzah meal
2 eggs	vegetable oil

Grate the potatoes either by hand or in a food processor. Grate the onion. Drain the liquid. Mix all the ingredients together except the oil. Heat the oil in a large frying pan. Drop about 1 tablespoon of the mixture for each latke into the pan, and fry over medium heat until it is crisp and both sides are golden brown. Serve with applesauce or sour cream.

Birmuelos

(makes 4 dozen)

These are sometimes filled with jelly and dusted with confectioner's sugar. (When frying, keep a bowl of water handy to rinse your hands between batches.)

2 packages active dry yeast	2 tbs. vegetable oil
3 cups warm water	6½ cups all-purpose flour
2 tbs. sugar	6 cups oil for frying
1 tsp. salt	Confectioner's sugar or honey

Combine yeast, water, and sugar in a large bowl. Let stand 5–10 minutes, until foam forms on the surface. Add salt, oil, and flour. Mix well to make a smooth, sticky dough. Cover the bowl with a clean towel, and allow to rise in a warm, draft-free place 1 hour or until doubled in bulk. Punch the dough down. Allow it to rise an additional 30 minutes. In a deep saucepan, heat the oil to 375° F. Break off 2-inch balls of dough (about the size of ping-pong balls) and drop into the hot oil, 3 or 4 at a time. Turn when golden on one side. When golden on the second side, remove with a slotted spoon and drain on paper towels. *Birmuelos* fry quickly, so watch carefully. Sprinkle with confectioner's sugar or honey, and serve.

From *Sephardic Holiday Cooking*, Gilda Angel (Decalogue Books, 1986).

Additional Chanukah Resources from the UAHC Press and Transcontinental Music

Celebrate Chanukah CD, Westminster Conservatory Youth Chorale.

The Chanukah Blessing, by Peninnah Schram, (2000).

Chanukah on the Prairie, by Burt Schuman (2003).

The Chocolate Chip Challah Cookbook, by Lisa Rauchwerger (2000).

The Complete Chanukah Songbook, by J. Mark Dunn and Joel N. Eglash, eds. (2003).

The Complete Book of Jewish Rounds, J. Mark Dunn, ed. (2002).

The Complete Jewish Songbook for Children: Manginot, Stephen Richards, ed. (1992).

Hanerot Halalu CD, Doug Cotler, prod. (1993).

The Jewish Home, Revised Edition, by Daniel Syme (2003).

Lights: Choral Music for Chanukah CD.

For more information on books please visit
www.uahcpress.com.

For Chanukah sheet music or more information on music,
please visit www.TranscontinentalMusic.com.